Popular Party Games

D1460639

Popular Party Games

Edited by Alison M. Abel

Illustrated by Ashley Pope

WARD LOCK LIMITED · LONDON

© Ward Lock Limited 1973

Paperback ISBN 0 7063 1041 1
Cased ISBN 0 7063 1040 3

First published in Great Britain in
1973 by Ward Lock Limited, 116
Baker Street, London, W1M 2BB
Reprinted 1974

Designed by Conal Buck

Text set in 11pt Plantin

Printed and bound by Cox & Wyman Ltd,
London, Reading and Fakenham

Contents

Introduction

Anyone who has ever organized a children's party will know that there is one key word never to be forgotten if the guests are to proclaim the occasion a success and the hostess to escape exhaustion and ragged nerves. Planning! The date, the time, the party fare, the decorations, the ages of the guests – all need careful thought. And once these are settled, one vital question looms. How to entertain the children? With games, certainly. But which games? In what order are they to be played? How can the party-giver break through the initial reserve with which all parties seem to start? How can she keep the children both happily occupied and quiet in that uncertain period immediately after a rich party tea has been consumed? What opportunities can she give her lively guests for burning up their overwhelming energy?

The answers to these questions lie in the following pages. The arrangement of the games described is designed to be of particular help to anyone faced with the task of planning a party programme. Classified by type rather than by age (since older children, despite their surface sophistication, will readily join in games with the small ones) each section in itself includes a wide variety of games suited to all ages and interests. In this way it is hoped that not only parents, but also teachers, youth leaders, church leaders and supervisors of brownie, guide, cub and scout movements will all find this book an invaluable guide to both little-known games and established favourites.

⚙ INDOOR GAMES ⚙

Many of the games appearing in later sections of this book are also 'indoor games'. Those here presented are wide-ranging in type and age-level, defying classification but too enjoyable to be omitted simply because they won't sit tidily under a specific heading. Word games, chasing games, acting games, games of skill – these and many more will be found here in plenty and variety. No organizer of children's parties need despair of occupying and amusing a lively, excited gathering of children when she can introduce them to such games as the Kipper Race, Butterfly Hunt, Fishermen, the Lucky Feeding Game, and the many others to be found on the following pages.

⚙ ADVERBS ⚙

One of the players, who later becomes the Questioner, withdraws from the group whilst the others decide upon an adverb. They will indicate the word they have chosen by the manner in which they answer the questions put to them. Suppose they have chosen 'sarcastically'; each player, on being questioned, must answer in a sarcastic manner. When the Questioner has guessed the adverb, another player takes a turn. The next adverb might be 'joyously', the next 'briefly', then 'dramatically', 'disagreeably', 'untruthfully', 'shyly', and so on. Sometimes the manner or expression of the players will indicate the word and sometimes, as in the case of 'untruthfully', the actual wording of the answers.

😉 SEAT SWOPPERS 😉

All the players sit on chairs in a circle except for one who stands in the middle. This player calls out which players are to change places, and while they are changing he tries to slip into one of the chairs. If he succeeds the one left without a seat takes his place in the middle.

The game is even greater fun if the player in the middle thinks of original statements to describe those who are to change places, such as: 'All change those wearing black shoes'; 'All change those who had an egg for breakfast'; etc.

😉 FISHERMEN 😉

This game is best played in heats of three or four players with a final for the winners.

You will need four reels of cotton. Tie a teaspoon securely to the end of the thread of each reel. Place the teaspoons on the floor at one end of the room and unwind the reels to reach the other end. Four players stand on chairs, each holding a reel. On the word 'Go!' they start winding the reels by turning them in their fingers (no overhand winding is allowed!). In this way they draw the teaspoons towards them. The first to draw up a 'fish' is the winner of the heat.

𝕾 SHOPKEEPERS 𝕾

If there are no more than eight players they can compete against each other. If there are more than eight, they can be divided into teams with a Manager and several assistants. Each player (or team) is given a card bearing the name of a shop: Hairdresser, Stationer, Greengrocer, Baker, Ironmonger, Draper, Florist, Grocer, etc. Hidden about the room or house are small tickets on which are written the names of articles sold in the various shops. Make sure there are the same number of articles for each shop; and as there may be some overlap in the articles for the Hairdresser's shop and the Draper's, mark these tickets with a small H or D. The players try to get together for their shops as many articles as they can in a given time. (If the game is being played as the team game, the Manager can receive the cards while the assistants do the hunting.)

The player who collects the most articles for his shop in the given time is the winner.

𝕾 BUTTERFLY HUNT 𝕾

Draw a simple outline of a butterfly on thin card. Cut out the shape, and using it as a template cut out a number of butterflies from coloured paper, the colour pages of magazines, or odd scraps of material. Place these about the room, never quite hidden, but matching colour to colour where possible so that the butterflies are less easily seen.

At the word 'Go' the players set out to collect as many butterflies as they can in the given time. The one with the most butterflies at the end of the game is the winner.

☺ PILLAR BOXES ☺

A game which tests the geographical knowledge of the players, Pillar Boxes will also provide a good deal of fun and racing about for older children.

You will need a number of shoe boxes. Cut a slit in each lid and write in large letters the name of a county on each box. Distribute the boxes round the house. Then, on small slips of paper – about six times as many as there are players – write the names of towns to be found in the counties you have chosen. You can have more than one slip bearing the name of the same town. Fold the slips to hide the names, and put them into a box on a table. This is the Sorting Office.

To play the game each player goes to the Sorting Office, takes a slip, writes his name on it, runs to find the county box for his town, and posts the slip. (The players can only take away one slip at a time.)

When all the slips have been posted, the boxes are collected and their contents checked to make sure the towns have been put with the right counties. The slips are then counted, and the player who has correctly posted the greatest number is the winner.

☺ FOUR'S A FAMILY ☺

For this game you can either use a set of 'Happily Family' cards or prepare cards yourself by writing sets of names on them, *e.g. Mr. Brown*; *Mrs. Brown*; *Miss Brown*; *Master Brown*. You will need as many 'families' as there are players. Take one card from each set, and distribute the remainder round the room. At the start of the game, give each player one of the remaining cards, face down. At the word 'Go' they turn over their cards, and set off to find the other three belonging to their families. The first to complete a family of four is the winner.

GIANT'S TREASURE STORE

A game for the very young, this can be played by small or large numbers of children. The giant is chosen and he lies sleeping on the floor, snoring realistically. Beside him is his treasure – buttons, beads, bangles, curtain rings, etc. The other children creep forward, but if the giant looks up at them they must stand quite still. Anyone seen moving drops out of the game. As the giant drops off to sleep again they continue moving forward. At last one of the treasures is seized, and the 'robber' starts back towards his den with the giant racing after him. If the robber is caught he drops out of the game. If not, he becomes the new giant.

(In the chair.)

GRANDMOTHER'S FOOTSTEPS

Another game for the very young. The players line up against the wall at one end of the room while the one chosen to be Grandmother stands at the other end with her back towards them. The players creep forward; but whenever Grandmother whirls round they must stop advancing and stand quite still. If she sees any of them moving, she sends them back to the starting line again. The first to touch Grandmother's shawl becomes the next Grandmother.

Giant's Treasure Store

☺ CINDERELLA AND ☺ PRINCE CHARMING

This is a game for a fairly large party. The children stand in a ring. Prince Charming is chosen and blindfolded. Cinderella is then chosen silently, and unknown to the Prince. The two children are placed inside the ring, as far from each other as possible. They call each other by name, but must not have any other conversation. When Prince Charming has caught Cinderella he has to guess who she is. If he guesses wrongly another Cinderella is chosen and he has to try once more. If he guesses correctly, two new children are chosen and the game starts again.

☺ PUSS IN THE CORNER ☺

This game for very young children is better played with a few rather than many, and requires an empty space in the centre of the room, with all breakable objects cleared away. Puss is chosen, and stands in the middle of the room chanting: 'Poor Puss wants a corner! Poor Puss wants a corner!' the others, who are standing in their corners, or dens, must now move, and if Puss is quick she will find herself a vacant den. The child left homeless becomes the next Puss.

☺ TOM CAT AND ☺ MISS MOUSE

One child is the Cat and another the Mouse. The Mouse

stands inside the ring, and the Cat outside. As the children in the ring move round they chant:

> 'What o'clock is it?'
> 'Just struck nine.'
> 'Is the Cat at home?'
> 'He's about to dine.'

At the end of the verse the Cat pops into the ring and the Mouse (who keeps as far away from the Cat as possible) pops out. The Cat must now follow exactly in the footsteps of the Mouse. The two chase in and out of the ring until at last the Mouse is caught – and eaten! Then another pair take the parts of the Cat and the Mouse.

☺ I WROTE A LETTER ☺

> I wrote a letter to my love,
> And on the way I dropped it.
> I dropped it, I dropped it,
> And on the way I dropped it.

One child is chosen, and given a letter. The other players are seated in a circle. The child with the letter runs round the outside of the ring, repeating the words over and over again and at one point drops the letter behind one of the players, who must pick it up and chase the dropper. The letter-dropper tries to reach the vacant place first, and if she succeeds, the child without a place in the ring becomes the next letter-dropper.

☺ SPINNING THE PLATE ☺

This is a good game for older children (of eight or nine years and more) who know each other well enough to remember everyone's name. One player stands in the middle of the ring, holding a large tin plate. He bends down and spins the plate, at the same time calling out the name of one of the other players. This child must run forward and catch the plate before it drops. If he is successful he then becomes the next spinner. A state of great excitement is generated as each child eagerly waits to hear his or her name called.

🎾 NOAH'S ARK 🎾

A game to amuse very young children. Two of the players are chosen as Mr. and Mrs. Noah. They stand at the door of the Ark. The rest of the children take partners, one partner being the 'Mr.' animal and the other the 'Mrs.' animal. Each couple in turn goes to the Ark, 'Mr.' acting the animal he has chosen to be, and 'Mrs.' (who does not know which one he has chosen) copying him as closely as she can. When they reach the Ark Mr. and Mrs. Noah ask: 'Who comes for a home in the Ark?' Mrs. Animal has to reply. If she gives the right animal name they go into the Ark but if she is wrong she and her partner are both drowned in the flood!

🎾 MYSTERY MIMES 🎾

Great fun for both players and audience this miming game is suitable for large or small numbers

Four players go out of the room. The leader then explains to the others that he is going to mime a short scene and outlines what this will be.

One of the players is called in and told to watch carefully as the leader performs his mime. Then a second player is called in to watch the first copying the leader's actions. This player then performs the mime for the third player and the third for the fourth.

The game can end in either of two ways. The fourth player may perform the mime, followed by the leader repeating his original movements. The performers will be amazed to learn what the mime was supposed to represent, and how much the mime changed as it was repeated.

Alternatively the fourth player, after watching the third miming the scene, must guess what it was supposed to represent.

Here are a few suggestions for scenes; the players will think of many more themselves:

1. Washing an elephant.
2. Buying a pair of shoes.
3. Writing a letter, sticking a stamp on the envelope, and posting it.
4. Bathing a baby.
5. Climbing a ladder and painting the ceiling.
6. Making a bed.

DUMB CHARADE

This is a firm favourite among older children. Divide the players into two equal groups. One group is the audience. The other group, the actors, go outside the room and choose the word they will act. If the children are quite young a nursery rhyme or pantomime title is the best choice. When the actors have chosen their rhyme they return to the room and mime it before the audience. If the audience guesses the rhyme or word they then become the actors and the actors become the audience. This is a useful game to suggest half-way through the party, when the children are quite tired but still full of party spirit and enthusiasm.

HOW GREEN YOU ARE!

One player is sent out of the room. The others decide on a particular action he is to perform, such as taking a book from a shelf and handing it to someone. When the player returns to the room the others begin to sing 'How green you are' (to the tune of Auld Lang Syne). When the player goes near the book shelf they sing more loudly. As he moves away the singing becomes softer. In this way they tell him how near he is to performing the action they have chosen. In a surprisingly short time he will realize what action he must make. It is then the next player's turn to go out of the room while the others decide on another action for him to perform.

VACANT CHAIR

This is a useful game for filling in a few minutes while another is being prepared – and it will be welcomed by those with surplus energy after a number of quiet games.

Arrange in a circle the same number of chairs as there are players. The players are seated with the exception of one, who stands in the middle. He must try to get into a vacant chair while the others try to prevent him by moving continuously round the circle from chair to chair. When he does manage to hurl himself into a chair, the player on his right goes into the centre.

KIPPER RACE

It is a good idea to let the players have a trial run at flipping their 'kippers' before starting the race. You will need a kipper, cut from tissue paper, for each child. At one end of the room space out a number of plates or saucers. The children line up at the other end, each with a fish and a magazine or folded newspaper with which to flip the kippers towards the plates. At the word 'Go' the players begin wafting the papers behind their kippers. Anyone touching the kipper with his magazine is out of the game. The first to land his kipper on a plate is the winner.

🦉 JIGSAW HUNT 🦉

For this game you will need as many pieces of different coloured or patterned paper as there are players. Cut the pieces into squares of different sizes, and then cut each square into four pieces to make a little jigsaw. Keep a 'key' piece of each jigsaw and hide the others about the room.

At the start of the game give each player a 'key' piece. The first to find the other three and put together his jigsaw is the winner.

🦉 RABBIT RACE 🦉

A game for all ages which causes great excitement and amusement, this race is best run in heats, with a final to select the winner.

Cut out three or four rabbits from cardboard and make a small hole in the middle of each. Thread a string through the hole and attach one end to a chair leg.

The players hold the other end of the string, and at the word 'Go' begin jerking the strings so that the rabbits move along towards the chair. The first one to get his rabbit down the length of the string is the winner.

BALLOON STICK

This is a useful game for a small party of young children. Choose two players and give them a balloon each and a short stick or piece of wood. In the centre of the room place a large basket or box. The idea is for the players to get their balloons into the box simply by using the sticks. They are disqualified if they use their hands or feet. The player who first gets his balloon in the box is the winner.

SHIPS ON THE OCEAN

This game is best played in a large hall. The players form four groups, one in each corner, with the exception of two who stand in the middle of the room and represent torpedoes. Each corner represents a country, *e.g.* India, Australia, Canada, Africa, and the players are ships.

On the word of command two sets of ships change places (*e.g.* India to Africa and Africa to India). While they are crossing the ocean, the torpedoes touch as many as they can. The players touched drop to the floor where they stay for the rest of the game. The game is finished when only one player, the winner, remains.

DONKEY'S TAIL

Draw a large, tail-less donkey on a large sheet of brown paper or wallpaper and fix it to the wall. The competitors are blind-folded and led up to the donkey. You can either give each child a piece of chalk to draw in the tail, or, if you have time, you can make tails out of coloured paper or wool and give one to each child to pin on the donkey. The player who gets the tail nearest to the right place is the winner.

Variations of the game include 'Putting the eyes on the giraffe', 'Drawing the baby's nose', 'Pinning on grandfather's moustache', 'Drawing the parrot's beak' – and any others you like to try. Instead of drawing the animal or bird you can use a picture cut from a magazine – provided, of course, you cut off the part to be drawn or pinned on by the players.

☺ MURALS ☺

This game is as amusing for the onlookers as for those taking part.

Cut brown paper or wallpaper into squares of about two feet, and fasten the squares to the wall with drawing pins or sticky paper.

The players are blindfolded and each is given a piece of chalk. They stand in front of their papers, and one of the onlookers chooses a subject for them to draw – such as a house, bicycle, ship, pig, etc., – within a time limit of one minute. The players are allowed to feel the edges of the paper before beginning their drawings.

When the time is up the players remove their blindfolds to admire their efforts, and the onlookers vote for the best drawing.

☺ GHOSTS ☺

A favourite with older children, this word-making game needs no 'props' and can be played not only at parties but also on any occasion when a long wait or tedious journey threatens boredom and bad temper!

Donkey's Tail

The players each have three 'lives'. The first player names a letter, and the next adds another letter, having a definite word in mind. The players continue adding letters in turn until one of them finishes a word. This player loses one of his lives.

Proper names should not be used and it is best to ignore three-letter words. If a player adds a letter that seems impossible to his neighbour, he may be challenged. If it turns out that the player has a real word in mind, the challenger loses a life. A player who has lost three lives drops out of the game.

JUMBLES

The disentangling of words that have the letters jumbled holds a fascination for most people, and there are various ways in which this idea can be used for party games.

The simplest way is to compile a set of names belonging to a class of objects, write each one, jumbled, in block letters on a piece of card, and display the cards round the room. The winner is either the first player to 'unjumble' all the words, or the one with the most correct answers after a given length of time.

Useful groups of names are: birds, animals, trees, flowers, countries, girls' names, boys' names, things found in the kitchen, garden, railway station, etc.

SLOGANS

A game to test the players' powers of observation – as well as being fun to play.

Cut from newspaper and magazines between ten and

twenty advertising slogans number them and display them round the room.

The players each have a pencil and paper. As they go round the room they note the number of each slogan and against it write the commodity to which it refers. You can mix easy and more difficult slogans, and vary their difficulty according to the age of the players.

(9) SHOPKEEPERS' (9) STORY

A game which results in some unexpected – and often very funny – incongruities. Each player is a shopkeeper, and announces the sort of shop he has decided to keep. The leader has ready a suitable descriptive article from a newspaper or magazine, with all the nouns struck out. As he reads the article, the players take turns in filling in the blanks by naming an object sold in their chosen shops.

(9) EMERGENCY! (9)

This game is most suited to a group of not more than a dozen players. One player is chosen as the Questioner. He leaves the room and thinks up a series of questions relating to various emergencies. Each question must begin with: 'What would you do if—?'

The rest of the players think up mishaps, adventures and accidents, and each having imagined himself in a particular predicament, whispers to his left-hand neighbour his solution for dealing with the situation – such as 'I should 'phone the police', 'I should throw it in the river', etc.

Now the Questioner returns and asks each player in turn: 'What would you do if—?' Each player must reply with the solution given him by his neighbour; the answers, often wildly unsuitable, causing much amusement.

🦉 IN THE RIVER 🦉

A useful game, this, needing no advance preparation, to be introduced at a moment when young players' surplus energy threatens the peace of the party!

The players stand in two rows, facing one another, about four feet apart. They are on the river bank, and the space between them is the river.

On the order 'In the river!' they jump forward. On the order 'On the bank!' they jump backward. The leader catches them out by mixing the orders, and saying '*On* the river!' '*In* the bank!', when, of course, they must stay quite still.

All who make a mistake, or wobble, drop out.

🦉 WOOL GATHERING 🦉

Cut up some wool into fifty or so three-inch lengths, using four colours – say, red, green, blue and brown. Distribute these about the room on furniture, ornaments, curtains, etc. At a given signal the players go 'wool gathering'. On the word 'Stop' they count their pieces, and are told that the brown pieces score 4 points each, the blue 3, the red 2, and the green 1. (Give the highest points to the colour that is hardest to see. This will probably be brown if it is the tone of the furniture.) The player with the highest total score wins the game.

⚇ DO THIS, DO THAT ⚇

Providing a quiet interlude after a more boisterous game, this is enjoyed by children of all ages. One child calls out commands beginning 'Do this' or 'Do that'. If he says 'Do this', the players copy his actions; if he says 'Do that', they don't. Anyone who performs an action on the command 'Do that' drops out of the game, and the last player left in is the winner.

⚇ LUCKY FEEDING ⚇ GAME

This exciting and amusing game for large gatherings has a particularly sweet ending!

The players sit in a circle round a small table. On the table are a large block of chocolate wrapped in six or seven sheets of paper, and a knife and fork.

The players take turns at throwing a dice on the floor. Each time a player throws a three or a six he goes to the table and begins to unwrap the parcel. As soon as another player throws a three or a six he jumps up and the first player must immediately return to his place in the ring while the second player continues unwrapping the parcel. When the block of chocolate is unwrapped the game continues in the same way, but the lucky players now use the knife and fork to cut the chocolate along the grooves and eat the small square sections. The game continues until all the chocolate has been eaten.

The players should be told that they may only cut and eat the chocolate *one small section at a time*. They should also be warned not to grab the knife and fork, which must be dropped immediately another player comes to the table. Any player who does grab at them is out of the game – and loses his chance of a taste of the chocolate!

☺ TILTING THE ☺ ORANGE

A boisterous game which small boys, in particular, enjoy. It is played in pairs, and if there are enough players to make it possible, it is a good idea to have about three pairs taking part at once.

Each player has in his right hand a tablespoon with an orange (or tennis ball) on it. In his left hand he has another spoon. His aim is to knock off his opponent's orange whilst keeping his own on the spoon.

Have several heats and then let the winners play one another.

☺ QUICK JUDGEMENT ☺

This game tests the observation and memory of the players, and is more difficult than it sounds!

Each player has a piece of paper divided into nine squares as shown below, and five buttons. The leader has a larger sheet of paper, similarly divided, and five buttons. The players sit at a table with their eyes closed, and their sheets of paper and buttons before them. The leader places his five buttons on any five of the squares. He then calls 'Look', and while he counts slowly to ten the players gaze at the diagram. The leader then covers the diagram with a handkerchief and the players place their buttons on their papers in the same positions as the leader's.

Those who place their buttons correctly score a point. Set a target of, say, ten points, the first player to reach this score being the winner.

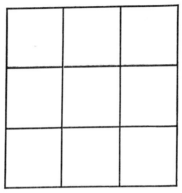

PENCIL AND PAPER GAMES

Many pencil and paper games are more suited to older children, but the little ones, too, will relish such games as The Queer Zoo, Dot-to-Dot, and Noises Off, while such games as Missing Letters can be adapted to suit children who have just mastered the writing of a number of basic words.

To provide a large number of guests with several sheets of paper each can be an additional and unwelcome expense when a party has already stretched the purse-strings to their limit. Remember that unwanted pieces of wallpaper can often be used, scrap pads bought cheaply from market stalls, and that for many games sheets of paper cut into quite small strips are sufficient.

Where the ages of the guests vary widely, remember to allow extra time for the younger, slower writers. The very young can be given another game requiring the minimum supervision, and selected, perhaps, from the 'Quiet Games' section of this book to keep them amused while the older ones are occupied with their own game.

🎶 NOISES OFF 🎶

This game needs careful preparation, but the fun it provides for the players makes time spent beforehand well worth while.

The players are each given a pencil and paper. They wait in silence while from behind a curtain or screen a number of different sounds are made. After each sound the players write down what they think made the noise they heard. (Make sure you keep a list of the sounds in the order they are to be made so that there is no doubt when the guesses are checked.)

Here are a few suggestions for sounds that can be made:

1. Gargling
2. Sharpening a pencil
3. Scratching a balloon
4. Pouring water
5. Sharpening a knife
6. Bouncing a ball
7. Jingling coins
8. Tearing paper
9. Bursting a paper bag
10. Winding a clock
11. Striking a match
12. Opening a newspaper

🎶 DOT-TO-DOT 🎶

This game can be enjoyed by players of all ages. Give a small sheet of paper and a pencil to each player. The players put six large dots on the paper, in any position they like. The papers are then collected, shuffled, and shared out again. They must now make a drawing in which the dots are joined together with lines forming the main framework of the drawing. When the drawings are finished they can be put on display for the players to vote for the best effort.

THE QUEER ZOO

The players sit in a circle, each with a pencil and paper. They first draw the head of an animal and fold the paper so that only a tiny part of the neck is showing. They then pass their papers to the left and continue by drawing the body of the animal with which they started. The papers are folded again, with just enough of the body showing to indicate where the legs are to be attached, and passed to the left. When the legs have been drawn the papers are folded and passed on for the feet to be added. Throughout the game each player draws only the appropriate parts of the body belonging to the animal he started with.

At the end of the game the papers are unfolded and passed round for all to admire.

MISSING LETTERS

Prepare a number of slips of paper, one for each child. On each slip print ten or twelve words with some of the letters missing, *e.g.* T – G E R. At the word 'Go', each player tries to complete the words and finish the list. The first to finish calls out 'Me first!' At this all the players must stop writing while the completed list is checked. If all the words are correct, this player is declared the winner; if not, the other players are given the word 'Go' again and can continue completing the words until another player calls out 'Me first!'

🎐 MIXED BAG 🎐

An idea for a small circle of players is to imagine that the contents of a schoolbag have been turned out on the floor. Write the names of the articles – with the letters jumbled – on good-sized cards and place them on the floor in the midst of the players who, in a given time, must write down what the objects are. The first player to 'unjumble' all the words or the one with the most correct answers after a given time, wins.

🎐 MISSING ADJECTIVES 🎐

To prepare this game take a passage from a book or newspaper. Strike out a dozen of the adjectives. Then dictate the passage to the players, saying 'blank' when you come to the adjectives.

There are two ways of finishing off the game: *a*) Leave players to fill in the blanks with what they consider the most suitable adjectives, and then read out the correct ones for checking; or *b*) give them the list of adjectives, but in a different order, and let them fill them in where they ought to go, in a given space of time.

🎐 HOW MANY WORDS? 🎐

The object is to make as many words as possible from a chosen word. Two-letter words should be ignored, and only the actual letters in the selected word must be used; that is to say, if 'a' appears once in the word, it must not be used more than once in any of the words that are made.

A suitable word would be one like 'Comradeship', and it

will be a surprise to those who have not tried this game to find what a large number of words can be extracted. After a 'trial trip' a system will be evolved, and there will be a hectic rush to write as many words as possible in the given time. Five minutes should be allowed.

The players then total their words, the one with the most words being declared the winner. Another method of scoring is for the players to read their lists in turn whilst the others strike out all the duplicates they have. Each player then scores according to the number of words on his list that have been thought of by no one else.

ANIMALS IN HIDING

Older children will enjoy this game in which they must find the names of animals hidden in a number of sentences. The letters of each name are used in the correct order and are not separated by other letters. Prepare a list of sentences for each player, and set a time limit of, say, five minutes.

Here, where the solutions are given, the game seems quite simple; nevertheless, few players will find all seventeen animals within the time limit.

Solution

1. The grass had been trampled, but he found a perfect dandelion standing erect.   *Ass, ape, lion*

2. He entered the cathedral.   *Cat*

3. Fear dogs me, and I still am beaten sometimes.   *Dog, lamb*

4. His eye lighted on keys that had been left behind on a seat.   *Donkey*

5. Tom, are you coming? The train will go at six o'clock.   *Mare, goat*

6. I am ill. Call Hannah, or send for a doctor.   *Horse*

34

7. You will never be a real force if you are so easily cowed. *Bear, cow*

8. He seemed to be worrying, or ill at ease, and just a tap irritated him, though it was in fun. *Gorilla, tapir*

9. You and Dinah are quite right; if you cannot transfer, return the tickets. *Hare, ferret*

10. The paths were like a maze, branching out in all directions. *Zebra*

THE THREE WORDS

Have ready three slips of paper for each player. Distribute the slips and ask the players to write three words, one on each slip of paper. The papers are then returned, placed in a hat and shaken.

The hat is passed round and each player takes out three slips. The players are then given a few minutes to write a sentence (of not more than twenty words) which includes the three words on their slips.

When the time is up, the players read out first the three words and then the sentence including these words. A vote is taken for the best sentence.

SNAPPY SENTENCES

This game for eight or more players lasts only a few minutes and can have some very amusing results.

Each player has a pencil and paper. Taking it in turns, the players call out a letter of the alphabet. As they are called, the letters are written down in the same order.

Only when the letters have all been noted are the players told their purpose. Each must write a sentence using words

35

beginning with these letters in the order in which they were called. Additional letters may be added, but it should be stressed that the fewer additional words used, the better the sentence will be judged. The players may not omit any of the given letters.

When the sentences have been completed the players read them out, and a vote is taken to decide which is best.

≋ WORD POWER ≋

This game is not only fun to play, but is also a useful 'filler' for short gaps in the programme or to occupy the guests while they are awaiting an entertainment.

The players are each given pencil and paper and are asked to write down as many items as they can belonging to a particular group or heading. (Suggestions for group headings are given below.) Set a time limit of, say, a minute. At the end of this time the players count the items they have listed. The one with the most items reads out his list, and if it is agreed that all the items belong to the group, is declared the winner.

The game can also be used when forfeits are required, the player paying the forfeit by calling out the items rather than writing them down.

Suggested headings
  1. Things that give heat
  2. White objects
  3. Names of singers
  4. Names of kitchen utensils
  5. Names of animals
  6. Names of birds
  7. Names of trees
  8. Names of flowers
  9. Names of sports and games
  10. Names of things with wheels.

 TEAM GAMES

Team spirit runs high in almost every child and team games have one important advantage over other types of contest – there is never one, individual winner; it follows that there is no isolated loser, either. The very young in particular find it hard not to feel – and show – disappointment, particularly when full of party excitement. At all costs situations likely to result in tears and tantrums are to be avoided, especially when dealing with little ones who are not in the consoling safety of their own homes.

Most team games need plenty of space. Make sure all valued possessions are cleared away, along with small side tables and sharp-edged furniture which could cause accidents as the youngsters race about the room.

ELEPHANTS

This game is as much fun for the odd ones out to watch as it is for those who are playing. Pin on the wall as many sheets of white paper as you have teams. Each team consists of six

37

players, who have to draw an elephant. At the end the non-players decide which is the best effort.

Number the members of the teams from one to six as follows: *ones* have to draw the head, *twos* the body, *threes* the tail, *fours* the trunk, *fives* the front legs, and *sixes* the back legs. When a number is called the players given this number come forward and draw the portion allotted to them. The numbers may be called out in any order, so that you might have the back legs drawn first, then the head, then the body, and so on.

※ ARTISTS ※

For this game you will need to prepare a list of about ten objects. These can be anything you like, so long as they are fairly easy to draw.

The players are divided into teams, each team having a pencil and a block of drawing paper. The leader is stationed in another room with the list of objects. At the beginning of the game the first player from each team goes to the leader who tells him the name of the first object. These players return to their teams and begin to draw the object. As soon as a member of a team guesses correctly what the object is, he runs to the leader who tells him the second object to be drawn. The game continues until one team has guessed all ten objects.

Although this is a drawing game you will find that the players need not be particularly skilful artists, for the objects are guessed from the roughest sketches.

✻ HURRY, WAITER! ✻

Two teams of eight players stand facing one another, with a good space between the players as well as between the lines.

The first player in each team holds a plate with a ping-pong ball on it. At the word 'Go' this player runs *in and out* down the line and back again, saying to each member, 'Here is your breakfast, madam (or sir)'. When he returns to his place he hands the plate to the second player who runs round the first player and then down the line, weaving in and out as before. If any player drops the ping-pong ball he must return to his place and start again.

✻ COTTON REELS ✻

The players stand in two teams, each behind a chair. On the chairs place four empty cotton reels, balanced one on top of the other. The first player lifts the reels, carries them right round his line and back to the chair. The next player then takes up the reels and carries them round the line; and so on. If a player drops a reel he must return to the starting point and begin again.

✻ MINIATURE ✻ EGG-AND-SPOON RACE

The players are divided into two teams and sit in rows along opposite sides of a table. Each player has before him a saucer and a teaspoon. The first players in each team have five peanuts in their saucers.

On the word 'Go' the first players pick up the nuts, one by one, on the handle end of their teaspoons and drop them into their neighbours' saucers. When all five peanuts have been transferred the second players begin passing them to their neighbours in the same way, and so on down the line. When the peanuts reach the end of the line they are passed back from player to player up the line. The first team to pass all their peanuts down the line and back again wins.

Very small children can play this game, using the bowl end on the teaspoon to pass the peanuts down the line instead of the handle.

✳ NOSE IN THE ✳ MATCHBOX

This game for older children gives a good deal of amusement. The teams stand in two lines facing each other. The leader of each side is given an empty matchbox cover which he fixes on his nose. The idea is to pass the matchbox from nose to nose right down the team. No hands are allowed, and if a player touches the box with his hands or drops it altogether it must be returned to the beginning of the line.

✳ HAT AND SCARF ✳ RACE

For this game you will need several hats (the funnier the better), scarves and pairs of gloves. The players sit on chairs,

Hat and Scarf Race

one behind the other, in teams of about a dozen. Give one set of clothing to the first player in each team. At the word 'Go' he puts on the hat, scarf and gloves, runs right round the chairs, then hands the clothing to the second player. Each player repeats the process in turn, making sure that the scarf is tied and the gloves put on properly before he runs.

✻ THE FISH POOL ✻

This team game for eighteen players is best played in a large hall. You will need three fans or rolled newspapers, and eighteen 'fishes' cut from coloured paper. (Use three different colours for the fishes, and cut six of each.) Mark a circle in the middle of the floor with chalk or string to represent a pool of water. The players stand in three teams, 20 to 40 feet from the pool, as if they were on three points of a triangle with the pool in the middle. Each team has six fishes of the same colour and a fan or rolled newspaper. The first player puts his fish on the floor and by fanning it (or waving the newspaper behind it) flips the fish into the pool. He then runs back to his team and hands the fan to the next player. If any player fans a fish out of the pool, he must fan it back before he can continue.

✻ THREADING THE ✻ BEADS

Have ready six saucers each containing twelve beads, six lengths of strong cotton knotted at one end, and six needles. Place the saucers in a row at one end of the room. The players take partners (a boy and a girl to each pair) and stand together at the other end of the room. Give each of the boys a needle and thread. At the word 'Go' the boys begin threading the needles while the girls run to their saucers, collect two beads, run back and give them to their partners. While the boys thread the beads the girls run to collect two more. The game continues until one player has threaded all twelve beads and has tied the necklace round his partner's neck. These two are the winners.

❋ DRESSING RACE ❋

This is a game for teams of six players each. For each team you will need a large paper bag containing six items of clothing (such as a hat, scarf, glove, shoe, belt, cardigan). Put the bags on a row of chairs. The players line up in teams behind the chairs. On the word 'Go' the first player takes an article from the bag, puts it on, runs to the other end of the room and back, and places the article on the chair. The second player then takes another article from the bag, puts it on, and runs. This is repeated until the sixth player of one team is home; his is the winning team.

❋ PASS IT ON ❋

This game is for two teams of, say, a dozen players each. The teams stand in two rows facing one another. At the end of each row is a chair on which are an assortment of objects, large and small. These have to be passed from hand to hand along the row in front of the players, then back down the line behind the players. Any object dropped has to be returned to the chair. When an object has been passed the length of the line and back again the first player places it on the floor. The first team to have all the objects on the floor is the winner.

The greatest fun comes when a player is dealing with two objects, one in front of him and the other being passed behind.

BURST THE BAG

For this game you will need as many paper bags as there are players. Divide the bags into two equal heaps and place them on chairs at one end of the room. The players are divided into two teams and stand in lines at the other end of the room. At the word 'Go' the first one from each team runs across the room, picks up a paper bag, blows it up and bursts it. Then he runs back to his team and touches the next player. This player then runs to burst a bag, returns to his team, and touches the third player; and so on. The first team to burst all its paper bags wins.

WORD-MAKING RACE

Prepare a list of words, of no more than five or six letters. Then, on pieces of card about six inches square, write the individual letters which make up the words. Make two sets of letters, one for each team. You need only duplicate letters in a set if they are used twice in one word. The two teams line up facing the leader, with a captain at the head. The captain takes a set of letters and gives one to each member of his team.

The leader then calls out a word from the list. Directed by their captains, the players holding the right letters line up so as to show the word. The first team to do this correctly scores a point.

The following is an example of how twelve letters (for teams of twelve players each) may be made into twenty different words:

The letters   A E I O U G L N P R S T   make:

REAP	LEAP	TEA	STALE
LONG	RING	GEAR	GRAIN
SUIT	SING	SONG	TRAIN
PEAR	SORT	PRONG	RUST
PALE	GRIN	SPEAR	PURE

✳ ALLITERATION ✳

This game will test the vocabulary of the players as well as their quick thinking. Write on slips of paper twenty letters of the alphabet, omitting *j*, *k*, *q*, *v*, *x* and *z*. Put the slips into a hat.

The players divide into two teams of up to ten players each. A player from the first side takes a slip from the hat, and in the space of half a minute has to call out as many words as he can beginning with the letter on the slip.

Then a player from the other side takes a letter. The process is repeated until all have taken part. A careful note is kept of the number of words called by each player, the side having the biggest total being the winner.

🎺 MUSICAL GAMES 🎺

There are many and varied games in which music plays an important part. In these, unexpected stopping and starting is usually required. If you have both piano and pianist, then this is ideal, especially if the pianist can also improvise and switch from tune to tune. Records can be used, but there should be a responsible person in charge, and even so it is best to use old records if possible as there is always the risk of scratches when interruptions are made during the course of its playing. If you lack both piano and record player, there are still the radio, simple musical instruments such as the recorder, tambourine, triangle, etc. – or even singing – to accompany the game.

🎺 PUZZLE FIND THE 🎺 RING

Adults as well as children enjoy this game. Arrange the group into a circle with one player in the middle. Tell him he has to try and see who has the ring when the music stops. The ring, which is on a long strand of stout wool knotted at the ends, passes secretly from hand to hand as the players allow the wool to slip quickly through their fingers. They must try to keep the ring itself invisible. Then the music stops. The player in the middle points to the one he suspects is holding the ring, and if he is right he joins the circle and the player 'caught out' takes his place in the middle. Very small children should be allowed to have some practice shots first as they may find the wool hard to manage.

🔔 MUSICAL HOTCH- 🔔 POTCH

A number of articles, beads, toys, nuts, or any other small items, are placed in the centre of the room. There should be one fewer items than there are players.

The children hop round the pile in time to the music. When it stops they each dive for an article. The one who fails to secure an object is out of the game. One article is removed, and the rest returned to the pile. The contest continues until there are two children and one object remaining. The one who takes this object is the winner – and keeps the article as a prize.

🔔 STATUES 🔔

The players each take a partner and dance round the room in time to the music. When the music stops they must become statues. If they are seen moving, they must sit down and watch the others; they can help with the decisions at the end of each round.

Musical Hotch-potch

🎀 QUEUE HERE 🎀

This game can be arranged to suit any number of players. On large sheets of paper (the back of a spare roll of wallpaper can be used) paint in block letters the names of types of shops; *e.g.*: Greengrocer, Chemist, Baker, Butcher, Ironmonger, Furniture Store, Grocer, Fishmonger. Fasten the sheets on to the walls at intervals round the room.

The players march round the room to music. When it stops, the leader calls the name of an article that can be bought at one of the shops – cabbage, nails, toothpaste, etc. The players race to queue up at the appropriate shop, facing the wall. The last in the queue, and any players who go to the wrong shop, drop out of the game. The music starts again and the remaining players continue their march round the room until the music stops and another article is called.

If there is a large number of players, they can march round the room in pairs. For a small number it will be sufficient to have only four or five shops, and the players can walk round in single file.

🎀 MUSICAL HUDDLE 🎀

While the music plays the players stand in a circle and pass round a duster tied into a ball.

The one with the ball in his hand when the music stops does not withdraw but stands in the middle of the circle. As the numbers in the outside ring are reduced, the players must make the distances between them equal.

Finally two players are left, and they must be at opposite sides of the cluster of players. 'A' must run round and hand the ball to 'B' and return quickly to his place. 'B' must then run round the other side of the cluster and give the ball to 'A'.

The winner is the one with empty hands when the music stops.

 # FAMILY REUNION

For this game you will need to prepare beforehand the same number of cards as there are players. On each card write the name of a member of a family. There should be three members to each family, *e.g.* Mr. Brown, Mrs. Brown, Baby Brown. If you have a set of 'Happy Family' cards you can use these instead, leaving out one member of each family.

Place the cards on a table and around the table arrange a circle of chairs, well spaced out. The players are grouped in threes round the chairs, two standing and one seated.

When the music starts the players begin walking round the outside of the circle. When it stops, they run to the table and each takes a card. They call out the names on their cards and re-group round the chairs in families of three.

The last three to form a family group are out of the game, and their cards are taken away. The other players return their cards to the table, the music starts again, and the game continues as before until the contest is between two groups. The first of these groups to form a family round a chair wins.

 # MUSICAL BOX-LIDS

Place at intervals upon the floor a number of cardboard box-lids (or pieces of cardboard) of various sizes. Players walk round in single file while the music is played. When it stops they must try to crowd on to the box-lids, even standing on one foot if necessary. All players touching the ground fall out of the game, and a lid is removed at each round. It is well to finish the game by having two players walking round one very small lid.

🎗 MAGIC CARPET 🎗

Another dancing game which children enjoy is 'Magic Carpet'. The children dance or jog round in pairs to a lively tune. They are told that somewhere on the 'Magic Carpet' is a 'Magic Patch', which has been previously decided upon by the hostess. Small prizes are awarded to the pair standing on, or nearest to, the 'Magic Patch'.

🎗 HIGH STEPPERS 🎗

The chairs are arranged in pairs with the front of the seats of each pair touching. They should be placed in an even line round the room.

The players march along in pairs to the music, stepping on to and over the chairs as they come to them. When the music stops any players who are partly on the chairs are out of the game and their chairs are removed. The game continues until only one pair – the winners – remain.

🎗 PASS THE PARCEL 🎗

A very small gift is wrapped in a very large parcel, with many separate sheets of different coloured papers, each tied with string. The players pass the parcel round the circle to music.

When it stops the player holding the parcel begins to unwrap it. Immediately the music starts again he must pass on the parcel. The player who takes off the last layer of paper is the winner, and keeps the gift as his prize.

MYSTERY PARCEL

A small gift is wrapped in a large parcel as in 'Pass the Parcel', but on each wrapping is written an instruction. When the music stops, the player holding the parcel reads aloud the message and proceeds to carry it out. Here are some examples: 'Hand to the tallest person', 'Hand to the guest with the longest hair'. If thought desirable, the *last* message can be 'Hand to the youngest person present'. It may be appropriate to single out some other guest for the special privilege of keeping the gift. Alternatively you can include instructions which are more like forfeits, such as 'Sing a verse of song', 'Hop round the ring', 'Imitate a cat washing.'

Another way of using this idea is to let it follow on another game. Present the parcel to the winner of the game, and tell him (or her) to read and follow the instructions. The parcel is handed on as before, but without music being played. The final instruction is: 'Hand to the original winner', and this gives it back to the player with whom it started.

MUSICAL POSTMEN

The players may either be seated or standing in a circle for this game.

Whilst the music is being played they pass round, in opposite directions, a letter and a small parcel.

When the music stops, the player holding the letter drops out. At the end two players will be left, passing the letter and the parcel backwards and forwards. The winner is the one holding the parcel when the music finally stops. He opens it, to find that it contains a small gift.

The player holding the letter opens it to find that it contains some simple instructions, which he has to carry out, such as 'Bow to the winner'.

MUSICAL ROCK

You will need a bar of rock and a wooden stick of the same size. Make up the rock into a strong parcel tied with ribbon or string. Do the same with the stick so that both parcels look exactly the same.

The players sit in a circle. When the music starts they begin passing the two parcels round the circle in opposite directions. When the music stops the two players holding the parcels drop out. The game finishes with the last two players passing the parcels backwards and forwards until the music stops and they open the parcels.

MUSICAL CARS

Write on postcards, in block letters, the names of parts of a car, such as BODY, WHEEL, ENGINE, DOOR, WINDSCREEN, BONNET, BOOT, etc. Write one word on each card and have as many sets of cards as there are players. Cut the postcards in halves and mix the cards, face downwards, in a box.

The players sit in a circle and hand round the box while the music is playing, each taking a card from the box. When the music stops they continue to pass round the box, but may not take out cards until the music starts again.

No player may hold more than two cards at a time. Unwanted cards are returned, face downwards, to the box. The first player to make a complete car part with his cards is the winner.

❦ MUSICAL RINGS ❦

This is a game to be played when there are a large number of players.

The players form themselves into groups of three, join hands, and dance round to the music. When it stops, the leader calls a number, say five. The players then break up and re-form themselves in groups of five. Those players who cannot join a ring quickly enough, and are left 'spare', drop out of the game.

❦ MUSICAL CHAIRS (1) ❦

Any number up to about twenty can play. There should be one chair fewer than there are players, the chairs being placed in a circle.

Players walk, hop or dance round the chairs in time to the music. When it stops the child failing to secure a chair is out. Another chair is then removed, and the game proceeds. The last left in wins the game.

If chairs are limited in supply, Musical Bumps is enjoyed just as much by young children. In this case, the child who is the slowest in falling to the ground when the music stops is out, but it is advisable to have a responsible person in charge so that there are no squabbles over who is out!

MUSICAL CHAIRS (2)

The chairs are arranged in the same way as for the last game, but the number of chairs is the same as the number of players.

At the start of the game the players each take a seat and memorize their positions. When the music starts the players run clockwise round the ring. When it stops they must carry on in the same direction until they have reached their *own* chairs. The last to reach his chair must remain seated for the rest of the game.

The game can be further varied by the person in charge of the music giving such instructions as: 'Right-about turn', 'Hop', 'Skip', etc.

 SINGING GAMES

You will find that nearly all children know both the words and the music of most of these games. The others will quickly pick up the words, and if no suitable tune can be found for less familiar rhymes they are equally effective if the children simply chant the words.

The repetition involved in many singing games has a particular appeal for younger children. So great is this appeal that many of the verses have survived for centuries, passed on by generations of small children until they have become part of a child's heritage, though the significance of references to contemporary events with which many began may well have been forgotten.

BLACKTHORN

> *Blackthorn! Blackthorn!*
> *Buttermilk and barleycorn;*
> *How many geese have you today?*
> *As many as I catch and carry away.*

One player, 'Blackthorn', stands facing a row of children, the

56

'geese'. The lines of the verse are sung or chanted alternately by the geese and Blackthorn. At the end of the verse the geese try to run past Blackthorn to the other side of the room while he captures as many as he can. The verse is repeated, and the captives help Blackthorn to catch more geese as they run past, The last player to be caught becomes the next Blackthorn.

 # HARK THE ROBBERS

Hark the robbers coming through,
*   coming through, coming through,*
Hark the robbers coming through
My fair lady.

They have stolen my watch and chain,
*   watch and chain, watch and chain,*
They have stolen my watch and chain,
My fair lady.

Off to prison they shall go, they shall
*   go, they shall go,*
Off to prison they shall go,
My fair lady.

This is a game which appeals particularly to small boys.

Two boys join hands, holding them up as an arch for the other players to tramp through. The first two verses are sung first by one and then by the other of the two boys. At the finish of these, the child then going through the arch is stopped, and the third verse is sung with gusto. The prisoner is borne off and given a choice between a golden apple or a golden pear. Boys often prefer a more gruesome choice such as 'Eaten by Lions', or 'Swallowed by Serpents'. At any rate, whichever fate the victim elects to face, he is then sent to prison behind one or other of the leaders, and when all are captured the inevitable tug-of-war follows.

HONEY-POTS

Honey-pots, honey-pots, all in a row,
Twenty-five shillings wherever you go
Who'll buy my honey-pots?

This is just one of several rhymes for the game of Honey-pots, which is ideal for a party of mixed ages.

One child clasps his hands under his knees while two others lift him by the armpits and swing him to and fro. If his hands remain clasped throughout the verse he is a good honey-pot; but if he fails to keep his hands clasped, he is a broken honey-pot and is swept away. Small children love this game, and the older, stronger children enjoy swinging the little ones.

GUESS MY TRADE

Here are three men from Botany Bay.
Got any work to give us to-day?
What can you do?
Anything.
Set to work then.

Three players are chosen as the actors, and between them they choose a trade. The other players chant the rhyme, then watch the three actors acting out the work of their trade. The one who guesses the trade correctly becomes a new actor and chooses two other players to join him.

58

Honey-pots

MUFFIN MAN

Have you seen the Muffin Man,
The Muffin Man, the Muffin Man?
Have you seen the Muffin Man
Who lives in Drury Lane?

Yes, I've seen the Muffin Man,
The Muffin Man, the Muffin Man.
Yes, I've seen the Muffin Man
Who lives in Drury Lane.

The players form a ring and join hands. One child, who is blindfolded and holds a stick, stands in the centre. The children dance round, singing the verses. Then they stand still and the child in the middle holds out the stick and touches someone in the ring. This player must take hold of the stick, and answer any question which the Muffin Man asks. He may ask: 'Is coal blue?', etc., and she must reply in a disguised voice 'Yes' or 'No'. Then the Muffin Man guesses who is answering him. He is allowed three tries, and if he guesses correctly the child who was touched takes his place in the ring.

DUSTY BLUEBELLS

When children are first introduced to this 'running and singing game' they are thrilled by it, and the difficulty is sometimes to stop them playing. The game can be enjoyed by all ages and is best played in the garden or in a large room.

In and out the dusty bluebells,
In and out the dusty bluebells,

Who is your master?
Pittery Pattery on her shoulder
  Pittery Pattery on her shoulder.
  (Jeannie) is my master.

One child is chosen as the leader while the others form a ring
holding hands and arching arms. As they begin singing, the
leader skips in and out of the ring. When they reach the last
line of the song she stops behind one of her friends and taps
her shoulder in time to the music. 'Jean' then leaves the ring.
She is now the leader, while the first child hangs on to her
dress. They run in and out of the circle as the children begin
the verse all over again. As the game continues the train grows
longer and longer and has greater and greater difficulty in
wending in and out of the circle, which has grown smaller and
smaller. The last one to be chosen becomes the leader next
time.

🧒 FARMER WANTS A 🧒 WIFE

The farmer wants a wife,
The farmer wants a wife,
Hey Oh me daddy Oh,
The farmer wants a wife.

The wife wants a child,
The wife wants a child,
Hey Oh me daddy Oh,
The wife wants a child.

The child wants a nurse,
The child wants a nurse,
Hey Oh me daddy Oh,
The child wants a nurse.

The nurse wants a dog,
The nurse wants a dog,
Hey Oh me daddy Oh,
The nurse wants a dog.

The dog wants a bone,
The dog wants a bone,
Hey Oh me daddy Oh,
The dog wants a bone.

The dog wants a pat,
The dog wants a pat,
Hey Oh me daddy Oh,
The dog wants a pat.

This game is such an old favourite that most children will know the words.

The farmer is chosen and he stands in the middle of the ring. The children in the ring dance round him, singing. When they come to the second verse, 'The wife wants a child', the farmer chooses a wife to join him in the ring. At the next verse the wife chooses a child, and so on. The climax of the game comes when all the players left in the ring rush forward to pat the dog. It is a good idea to stress at the start of the game that the dog wants only gentle pats, otherwise the unfortunate child may emerge black and blue.

THE GRAND OLD DUKE OF YORK

O the Grand Old Duke of York
He had ten thousand men,
He marched them up to the top of the hill,

And he marched them down again.
And when they were up, they were up,
And when they were down, they were down,
And when they were only half-way up
They were neither up nor down.

Most children will know the words and tune of 'The Grand Old Duke of York', and those who don't can still join in with the clapping and will soon pick up the verse.

The children take partners and stand facing each other in two equal lines. While the children sing and clap their hands to the music the pair at the top of the line join hands and skip with a running side-step down the line and back again. When they reach their place at the top of the line the two split up. One child marches down the back of her line and the other down behind hers. They meet at the bottom and the new top couple take their turn at skipping down the line.

QUIET GAMES

There comes a time in all successful children's parties when peace and quiet seem to the hostess the most desirable and least attainable haven. The fact that small children also welcome quiet interludes when their excitement threatens to overwhelm them, is often overlooked. A number of quiet games, introduced at appropriate stages in the course of the party, will save the disastrous consequences of excitement out-of-hand and frayed tempers.

The games in this section are invaluable for such moments. Plan the programme so that a quiet game follows a series of more boisterous, energetic ones; have a few quiet games ready for before the 'party tea' so that you can slip away to make the final preparations. Keep some in reserve for immediately after the children have eaten, too. If the party is of a mixed age group, arrange a quiet game for the younger guests to play while the older ones are occupied with a more complicated one. In the same way, the older children will be spared loss of dignity and boredom if they can quietly play together while the tiny ones enjoy their frolics – all those, that is, who don't find themselves energetically joining the babies, as many will do with vast enjoyment.

🐉 GOODIES 🐉

Children of all ages love this game – for obvious reasons. Prepare for each child a dish containing half a dozen 'goodies'. On each dish there could be, for instance, a square of chocolate, a raisin, a slice of banana, a nut, a small biscuit and a date.

The children are blindfolded, the dishes brought in, and one dish placed before each child, when they have eaten their 'goodies' their blindfolds are removed, and they must then write down what they think they have eaten.

It would be a pity for the smallest children who have not yet learnt to write to be excluded from this game. They, too, can join in, whispering to an adult what they think they have eaten instead of listing the items.

🐉 HEDGEHOGS 🐉

For all ages, and especially useful at small parties, this is an unusual game that requires little preparation. Give each child a fairly large and, if possible, oblong potato, a saucer of pins and a pair of small scissors. At the word 'Go' each child must pick up a pin with the scissors and stick it into the potato. An adult or older child slowly counts up to twenty. The winner is the one who has given the hedgehog the most spines when the counting reaches twenty.

🐉 MENAGERIE 🐉

A restful game which is particularly welcome immediately

Goodies

after the children have eaten their party tea, when romping games should at all costs be avoided. It has the added advantage of being one of the few creative, non-competitive games which has a calming effect on over-excited guests.

Each child is given four pipe cleaners and two small black-headed pins. With these they make a zoo animal of their choice. The completed animals can be displayed on a table, and each child can take his own animal home at the end of the party.

🖋 INVENTION 🖋

Rather more complicated than the last game, 'Invention' will absorb children of all ages for quite a while, and is an ideal game to keep them happily and safely occupied if you must leave the party unsupervised for any length of time.

Give each child a tray on which are placed: the skin of half an orange or grapefruit; a small piece of crêpe paper; a dozen pins; eight spent matches; a length of wool; a pair of scissors. (Other items may be added or substituted according to the oddments you have to hand.) The children may make whatever they like with the materials. They need not use them all. A surprising range of amusing and inventive creations will be produced and an added bonus of the game is that the children can take their works of art home with them.

🖋 SPILL-SPEARING 🖋

This game takes only a short while to play. It is useful for filling in time while another, more complicated game is prepared – and it is fun to play too!

You will need a quantity of wooden spills, cut into small

pieces, an empty matchbox and a long pin (hat-pins are best if you can find them) for each player.

The children sit at a table each with a heap of spills in front of them. At a given signal they begin spearing the spills with the pins and shaking them off into the matchboxes. Give a small prize to the player who collects the most spills in a time limit of, say, a minute.

✂ STEAL-A-STICK ✂

The children sit round a table. In the centre is a bag of spent matches. One of the children tips the contents into a heap. Each child in turn must now remove a match from the pile without disturbing any of the others. If any of the surrounding matches move while a player is taking a match he drops out of the game. This is a game which holds the attention of the children to the bitter end. The winner is the one who has the greatest number of matches in front of him.

✂ MATCHSTICK WORDS ✂

For this game you will need a quantity of spent matches. One child starts off by placing a match in any position he chooses. The next child builds on the first stick, the idea being to turn the original stick into a letter. Words are then built up in this way. When a player fails to see how to make a letter which forms part of a word, he or she falls out of the game. This is a game enjoyed by all children who have mastered the spelling of a reasonably wide range of words.

🦎 THE MINISTER'S CAT 🦎

This quiet sitting game is enjoyed by both children and adults. The idea is to describe the minister's cat by using all the letters of the alphabet one by one. For example, the first player begins by saying: 'The minister's cat is an *angry* cat'; the second follows with 'The minister's cat is an *amiable* cat'; and so on, until no player can think of another suitable adjective beginning with 'a'. They continue in this way through the alphabet until all the letters have been exhausted.

If it seems that the game will be too prolonged, you can decide on a limit of, say, six or ten adjectives for each letter.

🦎 I PACKED MY BAG 🦎

The children sit in a circle on the floor. The first begins: 'I packed my bag and in it I put . . .' and then adds whatever article he wishes, say a 'brush'. The next child starts off: 'I packed my bag and in it I put a brush and a skipping rope.' And so on. Anyone who forgets an item or makes a mistake drops out of the game. Some children are extraordinarily good at remembering, and the contents of one bag sometimes number more than thirty articles before the game comes to an end.

🦎 PELMANISM 🦎

This memory game is popular with all ages. The choice of articles and their number should, of course, be suited to the age of the players. Nevertheless, it is surprising how many articles even quite small children are able to memorize.

The children sit in a circle, either on the floor or on chairs. A large tray covered by a cloth or newspaper is then placed in the middle of the ring so that all the children can see it. They are told that under the covering are several objects. They will be given four minutes to look at them, and then the tray will be taken away, and at a given signal they must begin writing down as many of the articles as they can remember. The covering is removed, and after four minutes the tray taken away and pencils and paper distributed among the players.

The articles on the tray can be selected at random; or, to make the game slightly easier, they can be grouped under such headings as: 'Things found in the kitchen'; 'Things found in the garden'; 'Things I like to eat' etc.

You can either set a (quite generous) time limit in which the lists are to be completed; or you can allow the children as much time as they need to write down all the articles they remember.

✄ FEELING IS ✄ REMEMBERING

Fill a thick stocking with an assortment of about twenty familiar objects such as a lemon, safety-pin, thimble, cotton reel, matchbox, spoon, etc., and tie the stocking securely at the top. The players sit in a circle and the stocking is passed from player to player, each one being given a minute in which to feel the objects. The stocking is then taken away and the players write down all the objects they can remember. When they have finished their lists the stocking is opened and the items checked.

For parties of more than half a dozen, two identical stockings can be prepared so that the passing round does not take up too much time. If no time limit is set for compiling the lists, the players may begin writing as soon as they have passed on the stocking. In this way the first players to feel the stocking are not at a disadvantage in having to remember the objects for a longer period of time than the last.

🦢 SQUIGGLES 🦢

Give each player a piece of paper on which to draw four marks, or 'squiggles'. These can be of any shape, and drawn on any part of the paper. Having drawn their squiggles the players pass the papers to the left. They must now try to make from the squiggles either four separate drawings or one complete picture. For this game it is best not to award a prize or judge the results in any way. The fun of making seemingly impossible marks into a picture is sufficient in itself; and some players are obviously more handicapped than others as the complexity of the squiggles can vary enormously.

🦢 NURSERY DRAWINGS 🦢

Distribute among the players pencils and plain postcards, numbered consecutively. Now ask them to make a drawing to represent a nursery rhyme of their choice. When the drawings are finished display them round the room. Give each child a slip of paper on which to write the numbers of the cards and against these the names of the rhymes they think have been illustrated. Have a small prize for the one who makes the most correct guesses.

✂ NOISY GAMES ✂

All children love to make a racket, and when noise-making is a legitimate activity their cup is full! But the wild excitement that both generates and is caused by noisiness can be frightening for young children who feel threatened by total loss of control.

The games described here will give them the chance to let off steam within the confines of an organized game; their energies contained in a safe, acknowledged form, the young players will gain greater enjoyment, and will readily settle to more peaceful activities once the legitimate rowdiness comes to an end.

Even the hostess will find noisy games invaluable. Organized rioting is easier for her to cope with, too. A noisy game is a useful starter to a party, for the ice is soon broken and shyness evaporates once the young guests realize they can be their own, boisterous selves.

Many games described in other sections of the book do result in a great deal of noise; those given in the next few pages differ in that making a din is an essential part of the game rather than the side-effect of natural excitement.

✖ DOWN IN THE ✖ JUNGLE

Small children, especially boys, adore this game because of its unlimited opportunities for noisiness! The more children taking part the better, although any number from twelve upwards is sufficient. If twelve are playing three children are chosen as lions, two as elephants, four as tigers, and so on. Lions, elephants and tigers, etc. then jumble themselves up behind two base lines at opposite ends of the room. A hunter is chosen and he stands in the middle and calls out an animal name. The animals called then advance, trumpeting or roaring as the case may be, from opposite base lines. The hunter, approached from both directions, tries to grab as many animals as he can. Any beast caught helps the hunter in the next safari!

✖ FARMYARD FROLIC ✖

This is an amusing but extremely noisy game for a small party of up to ten children. When they are all sitting quietly round the room go up to each one and whisper the name of a farmyard animal (*e.g.* dog, cat, hen, cow, pig, horse, sheep, cockerel, duck, donkey). At the word 'Go' each child then makes the noise of the animal he has been given. When the noise becomes unbearable, ring a bell and shout: 'All quiet!' Then the children must write down as many of the animal noises as they remember hearing.

🌿 ANIMAL NOISES 🌿

A game for very small children, Animal Noises needs an adult story-teller who can invent and tell a good, amusing tale. The children sit at the story-teller's feet. She gives each one of them (or a group of them if there is a large number of children) the name of an animal. Then she starts her story. When she mentions 'hens' all the hens in the audience cackle; when she mentions 'dogs' all the dogs bark. The funnier the story, the greater the children's enjoyment of this sometimes extremely noisy game!

🌿 THE BEAN GAME 🌿

This is a very exciting and very noisy game. You will need a quantity of dried beans, scattered around the room. Divide the players into teams of six and ask them to choose one of their members as leader. Give each team the name of an animal.

The object of the game is for each team to collect as many beans as possible until all are cleared away. But members of a team must not *touch* a bean. They simply stand by it and make the noise of their animal until the leader comes to collect it.

The team whose leader has in his hand the largest number of beans at the end of the game wins.

❧❧❧ OUTDOOR ❧❧❧
GAMES

A large garden can be the party-giver's blessing. Provided the weather is reasonably good, many games can be played out of doors, giving the children greater opportunities for racing about and saving wear and tear on furniture and nerves. A few outdoor games will sharpen the guests' appetites for the party tea, over which many hostesses spend hours in preparation and which can sometimes be left virtually untouched by over-excited children.

The games described in the following pages have a timeless appeal and are equally suited to the playing field and school playground. Once the children have learnt the games they will become firm favourites, played again and again, at every opportunity and by children of all ages.

If you have several children yourself it is unlikely that your lawns are thick and green; but you may still have prize fruit trees and flower beds. Be firm about banning the children from these – and if you have a greenhouse in the garden, make sure that rag balls or balloons are used in ball games.

🦋 STATUES 🦋

This is a peaceful game which can be very pretty to watch. The children line up, and one is chosen as Mr. Sculptor. He goes up to number one in the line, grasps her firmly by the hand and whirls her round. When he releases her hand, she must strike a pose. With older children it can be arranged beforehand what sort of characters they are going to try to become. *i.e.*, historical, comic, tragic, etc. When all the children have been turned into 'statues', Mr. Sculptor tries to guess what each one is meant to be. Any child who moves after he has been 'sculpted' falls out of the game.

🦋 FOX AND GEESE 🦋

One of the players is choosen as Mother Goose, and one as Mr. Fox. The other children, Mother Goose's 'babies', line up behind Mother Goose, clasping each other firmly round the waist. Flapping her wings and sticking out her neck, Mother Goose leads her little ones all over the garden in an attempt to escape from Mr. Fox, who tries to pounce on the last baby in the line. When he does capture a baby, Mr. Fox leads her back to his den before setting out to capture another of Mother Goose's little ones. Very young children play this game with great gusto and enjoyment.

🦋 BUNNY HOP 🦋

All small children enjoy doing 'bunny hops'. In this game all but three of the players are 'bunnies'. They wait in one corner of the room while the three remaining children, the 'ferrets', wait one in each of the other corners. On the word 'Go!' the bunnies leave their burrows and hop about freely, while the ferrets remain quietly in their corners. At the word 'Now!', the ferrets go into action on all fours, and try to catch as many bunnies as possible before they reach the safety of their burrows.

🦋 HOW MANY TEETH, 🦋 MR. BEAR?

Mr. Bear sits gloomily inside a circle. The others advance and pertly ask him: 'How many teeth, Mr. Bear?' If the bear growls 'Two', or any other number, they are quite safe; but if he suddenly mumbles 'Twenty – very sharp', they must fly for home, for the bear is after them. All he touches drop out of the game.

🦋 TIGGLY-WIGGLY 🦋 SNAKE

This is a romping game loved by children of all ages, and is best reserved for quite spacious gardens. One child is chosen as the snake and given a home. At the word 'Go' he leaves home to try to catch something for his supper. When he catches his first victim, she must hold his hand, and the two then continue to chase and catch. Each victim caught takes the hand of the last victim, so that eventually the snake heads quite a long line. The last child to be caught wins the game.

❧ TRAIN TAG ❧

This is a good garden game to be played when there is an odd number of children. The children pair off to represent an engine and its coach. The odd one out is the 'spare' coach. At the sound of a whistle the trains start chuffing round the garden. The odd one out chases after them, trying to link himself on to one of the trains. When he succeeds the 'engine' of this train becomes the next 'spare' coach.

❧ ENGINES ❧

This is another train game, differently arranged from the previous one, and one which children greatly enjoy because there is so much shunting backwards and forwards.

The players stand one behind the other in two teams. These are the 'carriages'. Ahead of each team, on a marked spot at a distance of five or six yards, stand the two 'engines' with their backs to the carriages.

At the blow of a whistle the engines move backwards towards their carriages. When an engine reaches the line, the first carriage links on to him by placing his hands on the engine's shoulders. The two of them then go forward to the spot where the engine was standing at the start. Having reached this spot they shunt backwards again to pick up another carriage. This backwards-and-forwards movement continues until all the members of one team are linked together; this is the winning team.

🙣 SCRIBBLERS' RACE 🙣

Six competitors, the Scribblers, stand at one end of the lawn facing their six partners, the Guessers, who stand at the other end. The run between them should be as long as possible. Give each Scribbler a pencil and a card with the name of an animal written on it.

The Scribbler turns his card over, runs to his partner, and begins to draw the animal on the blank side of the card. As soon as his partner guesses what animal it is, he takes the Scribbler's pencil and writes the name on the card. The two then race back to the other side of the lawn, the first pair to arrive there being the winners.

🙣 TENNIS BALLOON 🙣

For this outdoor team game you will need a hoop, tennis racquet and balloon for each team.

The teams line up, one behind the other. One member of each team stands some distance away, facing the team and holding up a large hoop. At the word 'Go' the first player in each team runs towards the hoop, patting the balloon with the tennis racquet as he runs. When he reaches the hoop he pats the balloon through, catches it, and runs back to his team. The second player takes the balloon and racquet and runs to the hoop in the same way. This continues until all the players of one team have taken the balloon to the hoop and returned; this is the winning team.

🐜 DONKEY 🐜

Older children enjoy this game rather more than the little ones who have not yet fully mastered the art of ball-catching. The children form a large ring, fairly well spaced out. Somebody starts off by throwing the ball to the player on his left. Whenever a player drops a catch, he takes to himself one letter of the word DONKEY. A poor catcher will find himself collecting the letters very quickly – to the enjoyment of the others! As soon as he has earned all six letters he is a donkey, and drops out of the game.

For a shortened version of this game, take the word ASS instead of donkey.

🐜 MAGPIES 🐜

This contest can be begun at the very start of the party, with no particular time set aside for it, the players gathering items in the odd moments between games, or when they spot something to add to their collection. Alternatively, you can gather together all those who wish to enter and set a time limit of, say, ten minutes.

Give each child an empty matchbox. It is a good idea to write each child's name on his box to avoid confusion at the end. The idea is for the children to collect as many items as they can to fit into the boxes. At the end of the party the matchboxes are gathered together and placed on a table with their contents emptied in front of them. The child who has collected the highest number of objects is the winner and receives a small prize.

❦ MINIATURE GARDENS ❦

A game particularly suited to summertime, a miniature garden competition is not only enjoyable for the players, but can also have some delightful results.

You will need some old dinner plates, tin plates or shallow bowls, with a fairly thin layer of soil on each. Give the players a plate each and ask them to make a miniature garden from flowers, leaves, grasses, stones, etc. Set a time limit at the end of which the players bring their gardens together to be judged.

If you have any prize plants in the garden which you don't want touched, warn the players about these at the start – or, better still, place small cards against the plants bearing the words 'Please do not touch!'

A variation of this game is 'Egg-cup Posies' in which the players are provided with egg-cups and asked to arrange a posy of flowers.

Miniature Gardens

GARDEN PARTY GAMES

If you have a fairly large garden you can make it a special feature at a party, presenting a number of games and contests in the same way as those played at garden parties and fêtes, and encouraging the guests to wander from game to game as they please. You can develop the theme further and make the whole party an outdoor one, arranging the refreshments on a trestle table in one corner with chairs and mats set around for the children to sit on while they eat.

There are a wide variety of games suitable for this kind of entertainment, ranging from egg-and-spoon, potato, sack, obstacle and three-legged races, to competitions and guessing games. If you want to make sure that no one monopolises a particular game, give each guest several coloured discs to represent 'entrance fees' for each game or competition.

Whether you are planning to hold the entire party out of doors, or only a small part of it as one feature in a variety of entertainments, make sure that you either have alternative games planned or can easily transfer most of the garden games to the house should the weather let you down.

❧ BOTTLE RINGING ❧

You will need six narrow-necked bottles, and six canes each with a length of string and a large ring attached.

Stand the bottles in a row with a good space between each. Six competitors line up opposite the bottles holding the canes. On the word 'Go' they begin trying to drop the curtain rings over the necks of the bottles. The first to succeed is the winner.

❧ BOTTLE FILLING ❧

For this contest you will need a large bowl of water set on a table, and a teaspoon and small bottle for each player.

The players stand round the table and on the word 'Go' they begin transferring water from the bowl to the bottles with teaspoons. The first to finish filling his bottle is the winner.

❧ AIMING STRAIGHT ❧

You will need a bun tin with six small hollows, numbered from one to six, and a small rag ball or woollen pom-pom.

About half-a-dozen players take part in each round, paying one counter as an entrance fee. They take it in turns to throw the ball into the numbered hollows, and the one with the highest score either wins a small prize or has his counter returned to him. If two or more players have the same score they play against each other until one emerges as the winner.

Bottle Ringing

❧ THREE BOXES ❧ CONTEST

Place on the ground three bowls of graded sizes, one inside the other. Set a marker a short distance from the bowls for the players to stand behind.

The players are each given five nuts, dried peas, or similar objects, which they take turns to throw into the bowls. The middle bowl scores five points, the second bowl three, and the outer bowl one point. Set a target of, say, fifteen points and announce the first player to reach this target the winner. Alternatively the players can each have three rounds, the one who scores the highest number of points being the winner.

❧ BUTTON STRINGING ❧

Two or three competitors at a time gather round a big bowl of buttons. Each has a thread with a button tied at the end as a stopper. Set a time limit of, say, three minutes. The player who has threaded the most buttons in the given time is the winner.

❧ PEA RACE ❧

The competitors each have before them a straw, a saucerful of dried peas, and a bowl. At the word 'Go' they place their straws in their mouths, and by breathing in pick up the peas from the saucer and transfer them to their bowls. The one who has picked up the most peas in a given time limit of a minute wins.

❀ CRAZY GOLF ❀

In this game the players compete in pairs. Mark a starting line on the ground and a second line a few yards beyond it. Give each player a tennis ball and a matchstick.

The two players stand behind the starting line with their tennis balls behind them. On the word 'Go' they begin propelling the tennis ball forward by means of the matchstick. When they reach the second line they turn and propel the balls back to the start. If a player touches the ball with his hand or foot he must return to the starting line and begin again.

The game can be made more difficult – and more amusing to the onlookers – if a few obstacles and hazards are placed on the course, such as crosses for points to be avoided and parallel lines through which the ball must be steered.

❀ MYSTERY ❀ MATCHBOXES

Put into 8 matchboxes a quantity of the following materials:

1. Pins
2. Peas
3. Rice
4. Matches

5. Paper clips
6. Tintacks
7. Currants
8. Sand

Number the boxes. Tell the competitors what the contents of the boxes are and let them make a note of them. Then they have to shake the boxes, and decide which contains which articles.

GUESS HOW MANY

Arrange on a small card table a collection of oddities, *e.g.* a jam jar with a number of small sweets in it, a pin-cushion with some pins, a box of buttons, a bundle of pencils, a jar filled with beans. These should be lettered. The children are told to write down on their slips of paper the letters A, B, C, D, corresponding with the letters on the oddities. They then walk round the table, and after a brief glance at the items, write down against each letter the number of articles they think each oddity contains. The game can be played by very small children because only a knowledge of the alphabet and numbers is needed. The prize is awarded to the child with the most correct list, *i.e.* one mark is given in each case to the player whose guess is most nearly correct, and then the marks are added up.

♦♦♦♦♦ **TREASURE** ♦♦♦♦♦ **HUNTS**

Treasure hunts are exciting for all children – and many adults enjoy them, too! They can be adapted for indoors, out of doors, for the very young, for older children, and can be related to the central 'theme' of a party. Easter Egg hunts, for example, are a particular favourite at Easter parties. The eggs can be hidden either round the house or in the garden. To ensure that each child ends up with an egg, give the players a colour and tell them to look for an egg wrapped in that colour. Any other eggs they find must be left in their place, and no one may tell another player where he has seen a hidden egg. If the party is too large for each guest to have his individual colour, write each child's name on a gift tag and attach the tags to the eggs before hiding them. For a mixed age group party, place the eggs intended for the younger children in the more prominent places, leaving it to the older children to search the higher and more unlikely spots.

Older children enjoy a treasure hunt in which a clue, or series of clues, leads them to a single treasure. The clues can be given in a variety of ways.

1. You can cut from newspapers or magazine pictures of articles the initial letters of which form the letters of the clue word. For example: supposing the treasure is hidden in the bathroom. The pictures could then be of a bed, apple, tricycle, hat, rocket, orange, oaktree, mouse. (They should not be displayed in this order.)

2. A key word can be used as above, but this time the letters of the word are jumbled, either on a single piece of paper or on separate cards hidden about the room. With this second method, the players must hunt for the letters, and on finding them they jot the letters down on paper, leaving the cards themselves in place.

3. The clue can be a whole sentence using as many words as there are players. A clue could be, for example:

'Here soap and water makes me clean;
And treasure trove waits to be seen.'

In this case each word of the clue is written on a separate card and the cards pinned to the players' clothing. The players are given pencil and paper, and having noted all the words they must first work out their correct order and then the place to which the clue is directing them.

4. If the house or garden is large and rambling, a series of clues can be used, each one directing the players to the next and, finally, to the treasure. The players can each have a complete list of clues and work their way through the house until they reach the treasure. Alternatively, the clues may be placed around the house, and in this case the players are given the first clue directing them to the spot where the second clue is hidden.

For any treasure hunt out of doors, it is of course sensible to warn the children beforehand of any prize flower beds they must not scrabble around. To further ensure the safety of *your* treasures, place notices bearing the words NO TREASURE HIDDEN HERE at places the children are to avoid. Make sure, too, that garages and garden sheds where sharp tools, delicate plants. etc., are housed are firmly locked. For an indoor treasure hunt do the same for any rooms, cupboards, and drawers the players are to avoid, and for dangerous stairways and dark passages.

❧ PLANNING THE ❧ PARTY

Once the date of the party has been fixed you can begin to make the plans which will ensure its smooth running and the guests' enjoyment, as well as minimising your own problems. Although most children's parties are held in the afternoon, a morning party can be a great success among tiny children who can become crotchety when overtired and deprived of their afternoon's rest. A simple lunch can be prepared, although even this is not essential, for milk, fruit juices, and a selection of biscuits are sufficient for very small children.

It is best to send out written invitations so that essential details are not forgotten and you can keep a record of the children invited. As well as the date and starting time, include such details as whether this is to be a birthday party (to save embarrassment as to whether small gifts might be brought); if the party is to have a special theme for which appropriate dress is required; the kind of meal to be provided (tea and buns, barbecue, full scale tea, etc.)

There is no need to buy special invitation cards. Plain postcards, with a small decoration cut from a magazine and pasted on one corner can be as attractive as printed cards.

You can buy sheets of coloured card from most stationers, and these, cut into an interesting shape (an egg for an Easter party, a witch's hat for a Hallowe'en party, a star or Christmas tree for a Christmas party) make very effective invitation cards. Write the details in bold, contrasting felt-tip pen. You can also cut fairly thick white paper to the size you want and let your child make a decorative border with potato cuts, stencils, or gummed coloured shapes.

Some children seem to have the most active social lives, with parties a regular – almost weekly – occurrence. To make your party less 'run of the mill' you can plan it round a central theme. Fancy dress parties are the most well-known of these, and very popular they are, too, although they can sometimes mean added time and expense for the mothers who must devise the costumes. A variation of the fancy dress party which is less troublesome for parents is a 'tramps' party'. The guests appear in their oldest clothes, the effect preferably enhanced by patches tacked to their clothing, battered hats, odd socks and baggy trousers tied with string.

Hallowe'en parties are a splendid way of brightening the beginning of winter. Make masks for the guests, lamps from hollowed turnips or melons with candles set inside, and decorate the room with witches cut from black card, decorated with sequins and suspended from light fittings, doorways and windows by strong black thread.

Other seasonal celebrations include the traditional Christmas party, and the less common Easter and Midsummer parties. You can celebrate both world and local events with an appropriate party. A 'space party' could coincide with a space flight, with games, decorations and food appropriately selected and named. The success of a local football team can afford a 'football' theme for your party, with the team's colours used for decorations and the walls hung with pennants and rosettes.

If all these aspects of the party, together with the programme of games to be played, are planned and prepared well in advance, then the occasion will not only prove to be a great success with the young guests but, far from being the chore so many parents feel children's parties to be, will also be an event which you, too, can enjoy.